Table of Contents

Moroccan Cooking: The Easy Way

For more information, please email us at info@flavorsofmorocco.com

Cover and interior design: Adina Cucicov, Flamingo Designs
Front cover picture: Nadia Stoti

www.cookingwithalia.com

Essential Moroccan Ingredients

Smen

Smen is a traditional butter-based cooking oil made of clarified aged butter. Smen is considered the main flavoring ingredient in Morocco and is used to enhance the flavors of many Moroccan dishes such as tajines and couscous. It is very similar to Indian ghee.

Making Smen:

The butter is brought to a boiling point, then is strained and salted before it curdles. The resulting grease can be flavored with herbs such as dried oregano leaves before being poured in a clean jar and stored in a cool place for at least 30 days.

Tips:

If you are using smen when cooking your meal, do not add additional salt without tasting it first.

Argan Oil

Argan oil is an oil produced from the kernels of the Argan tree. It is used in Morocco both for culinary and beauty purposes.

Important information about Argan oil:

1. **Where does it grow?**
   Argan oil is considered 'Liquid Gold'. It is made from the nuts of the Argan tree that grows almost exclusively in southern Morocco. If you drive by that region you can spot goats up in the Argan tree feasting on the fruit!

2. **A beauty product?**
   Argan oil is exceptionally rich in vitamin E, carotenes, essential fatty acids, etc. It is believed to help all sorts of skin conditions such as dry skin, acne, wrinkles, and so on. Moroccan women use it as a beauty product on their skin, hair and nails. Nowadays, you can find many commercial beauty products made of Argan oil.

3. **Culinary oil?**
   In Morocco, Argan oil is used in many recipes including couscous, tajines, and salad dressings. The simplest recipe is to dip grilled bread in Argan oil and honey, and eat it as part of the breakfast meal.

Interesting Fact:

Around 21 million of Argan trees grow between the towns of Essaouira and Agadir, and cover an area of around 700,000-800,000 hectares.

Ras-el-Hanout

Ras-El-Hanout, literally meaning the 'head of the shop' in Moroccan, is a popular Moroccan blend made of the best herbs and spices that the spice merchant has to offer. Each shop has its own unique 'secret' blend that can contain more than 30 different ingredients. Typically, Ras-El-Hanout would include spices such as cardamom, clove, cinnamon, paprika, coriander, cumin, nutmeg, peppercorn, and turmeric. It is mainly used in specialty tajines such as 'Mrouzia' (the sweet lamb tajine prepared during Eid) and adds an aromatic and enticing flavor to chicken or fish.

Important:

If you are serving a specialty tajine to a pregnant woman or nursing mother, make sure to not use Ras-El-Hanout because some of its components can be harmful (e.g. lavender leaves, which are a uterine stimulant.)

Rose Water

Rose water is the distilled water of roses. It is a must in every Moroccan kitchen. Rose water has a lovely scent and is used to flavor desserts and juices. Moroccan women also use it as a face toner to smooth and refresh the skin.

Orange Blossom Water

Orange blossom water is distilled water that contains the essential oils of the orange blossom. It is considered the primary flavor for Moroccan pastries and other main dishes such as sweet tajines. As with rose water, Moroccan women use orange blossom water for therapeutic purposes such as aromatherapy and skin care.

Preserved Lemons

Preserved lemons are one of the main condiments of Moroccan cuisine. The flavor of pickled lemons is very different from just the juice or the zest and adds a uniquely Moroccan taste to all dishes wherever lemon is called for.

Prep: 15 minutes; Preserve: 4-6 weeks

Ingredients:
Lemons
Salt
Glass jar

Steps:

1. Sterilize your glass jar by cleaning with hot water and soap. Then without drying the jar, put it in the oven at 350°F for 30 minutes.
2. Make a vertical cut half way through the lemon. The two halves should remain attached at the bottom of the lemon.
3. Turn the lemon upside down and cut the lemon vertically at a 90-degree angle to the first cut, halfway through the lemon. You will end up with 4 pieces that are still attached in the middle.

4. Pull apart the slice that you just made and add 1 teaspoon of salt to each.
5. Pack the lemons tightly in the jar until no space is left in the jar. Sprinkle some salt in the jar.
6. Put a lid on the jar and keep it at room temperature in a dark closet or cabinet for a month.
7. Check the jar during the first 3 days to verify if the juice produced by the lemons covers the top of the lemons. If the lemons are not covered with juice, add fresh lemon juice to the jar until the top lemons are covered. Put the lid back on the jar and preserve for 4-6 weeks.

Serving:

Rinsing the lemons: Preserved lemons can be used in tajines and salads. If you are using the lemons in a salad, rinse them to reduce the amount of salt. If you are using them in a tajine (Moroccan stew), you can choose to rinse the lemons or not, depending on the amount of salt that you have already put in the tajine.

Using the lemons: When using preserved lemons in a salad, dice the lemons and use both the pulp and the skin. However, use only the pulp when cooking the lemons in a tajine. Because the skin can make the tajine bitter, reserve it for decoration of the dish. This decoration lets diners know that the tajine was made with preserved lemons.

Tips:

Preserved lemons are actually pickled fruit. You can experiment with different flavors of the basic preserved lemon recipe by adding a tablespoon of spices like coriander seeds, cloves, cinnamon stick, peppercorn, or bay leaves.

Moroccan Cabbage Salad

Moroccan Cabbage Salad combines delicious tangy and spicy flavors. It can be served hot or cold, and goes best with bread! This dish can also be a perfect dip for a picnic.

Makes: 4 servings; Prep: 5 minutes; Cook: 40 minutes

Ingredients:

1 cabbage (approximately 2 pounds)
1/4 cup of chopped cilantro
1/4 cup of chopped parsley
1 tablespoon of cooking oil
1 teaspoon of crushed garlic
1 teaspoon of paprika
1 teaspoon of cumin
1 teaspoon of salt (to taste)
1/4 teaspoon of pepper (to taste)
1 teaspoon of vinegar (or lemon juice)

Steps:

1. Cut the cabbage into large pieces.
2. Put the cabbage in boiling water for 20 minutes. Once the cabbage is cooked, drain the water from the cabbage.
3. On medium heat, drizzle the oil in your pan and add the cabbage. Mash the cabbage for few minutes with a wooden fork.
4. Add all the spices, except the parsley and cilantro, to the cabbage and continue mashing it for 10 minutes.
5. Add the parsley and cilantro to the cabbage, and continue mashing it for 15-20 minutes until you get a smooth consistency.
6. Taste the cabbage and adjust the spices according to your taste. Add the vinegar (or lemon juice). Mix well.

Serving:

The cabbage salad is served hot or cold with bread. Enjoy!

Tips:

In a hurry? Use a hand-held mixer to mash up the cabbage quickly and mess-free.

Moroccan Carrot Orange Salad

This unique salad blends the sweetness of orange juice and the warmth of cinnamon with the crispiness of carrots. The orange blossom water gives it a special Moroccan touch. In Morocco this salad is served as a starter, a side dish, or a refreshing ending to a meal. It is a refreshing treat on hot summer days and can be a colorful, brightening addition to a winter menu.

Makes: 2 servings; Prep: 10 minutes

Ingredients:

2 cups of finely grated peeled carrots
1 cup of orange juice
1 teaspoon of orange blossom water
1/2 tablespoon of sugar
A pinch of cinnamon powder

Note: Feel free to adjust the measurements to your taste.

Steps:

1. Mix all the ingredients together in a bowl.
2. Refrigerate the salad for few hours before hours before serving.

Serving:

Serve the salad cold.

Variations:

If you add more orange juice and blend all the ingredients together, you will get a wonderful refreshing orange-carrot smoothie!

Zaalouk

Zaalouk (eggplant tartar) is an authentic Moroccan cooked eggplant and tomato salad that is served as a dip with bread. It can be eaten hot or cold. The smooth texture of this cooked salad and the winning spice blend make this dish a favorite even for people who usually do not enjoy eggplant.

Makes: 3-4 servings; Prep: 30 minutes; Cook: 30 minutes

Ingredients:
1 large eggplant (1 pound)
3 tomatoes peeled and diced (1 pound)
1/4 cup of chopped parsley
1/4 cup of chopped cilantro
1 teaspoon of vinegar
1 - 2 tablespoons of olive oil
1 teaspoon of crushed garlic
1 teaspoon of paprika
1 teaspoon of cumin
1/2 teaspoon of salt (to taste)
1/4 teaspoon of pepper (to taste)

Steps:

Steps to prepare the eggplant:

1. Peel and dice the eggplant. You can either peel off all the eggplant skin or leave half of it on, depending on your taste.
2. Boil the eggplant cubes in salted water for 20 - 30 minutes.
3. Using a colander, drain the eggplant cubes and press them with a spoon until all excess water is released.

Steps to prepare the Zaalouk:

1. On medium heat, add the tomatoes, eggplant cubes, olive oil, garlic and spices to your pan and cook them for 30 minutes.
2. Crush the eggplant and tomatoes with a wooden spoon while they are cooking to create a puree.
3. In the last 5 minutes of cooking, add the vinegar to the eggplant and tomatoes puree. Mix well.

Serving:

Zaalouk is served either hot or cold, with bread. Enjoy!

Variations:

For more flavors, you can steam the eggplants instead of boiling them. Also, you can add other vegetables such as zucchini or bell peppers, which you cook in a pan until they become tender before adding and mashing them with the rest of the ingredients.

Moroccan Tortilla

Tortilla is a Spanish dish made of eggs, potatoes, and onions. It has nothing to do with Mexican flour or cornmeal tortillas. The Spanish tortilla has been adapted to Moroccan kitchens with some additions such as parsley, cumin, and paprika.

Makes: 4 servings; Prep: 45 minutes

Ingredients:

4 Potatoes
1 Small onion, finely chopped
5 Eggs
1/4 Cup finely chopped parsley
2-3 Tablespoons of olive oil
1/2 Teaspoon paprika
1/4 Teaspoon cumin
1 Teaspoon salt (or to taste)
1/4 Teaspoon black pepper (or to taste)

Steps:

1. Peel the potatoes and cut them into small cubes.
2. On medium heat, drizzle half of the oil onto your pan and add the onions. Add a pinch of salt to the onions and stir well. Let the onions cook for 5 minutes.
3. Add the potatoes, spices and the rest of the oil to the pan. Cover the potatoes and let them cook on medium heat until the potatoes are tender. Remember to stir the mixture from time to time.
4. When the potatoes are almost cooked, add the parsley and let the mixture cook a few more minutes.
5. Transfer the potatoes to a separate bowl.
6. Beat the 5 eggs in a small bowl then add them to the potatoes. Mix well.
7. Pour the potato and egg mixture back into the pan. Shake your pan to even out the mixture. You want the tortilla to have an even consistency throughout.
8. Cook the tortilla at medium heat for few minutes. When the edges start to get firm, push them away from the pan with your spatula just to loosen the tortilla from the edge of the pan.
9. Put a plate over your pan and flip them so that the tortilla falls onto the plate. Slide the tortilla back into the pan so that the uncooked side is against the pan.
10. Cook the other side of the tortilla for few minutes. Push the edges of the tortilla away from the pan with your spatula.

Serving:

Serve the tortilla immediately.

Tips:

If flipping the tortilla intimidates you, try this alternative. After letting one side of the tortilla cook for 3 minutes, put the pan (make sure it is oven safe!) in the oven at 400°F for 5 minutes. After the 3 minutes, turn on the broiler and let the tortilla cook for another 3 minutes.

Moroccan Lentils

This highly nutritious lentil dish will warm you during the cold winter days and can be served as a starter or light dinner. It is an easy and quick recipe that fits perfectly in a busy schedule.

Makes: 4 servings; Prep: 10 minutes; Cook: 40 minutes

Ingredients:

9 oz of lentils, soaked in water for few hours
1 onion, thinly sliced
1 tablespoon of finely chopped cilantro
1 tablespoon of finely chopped parsley
2 tablespoons of olive oil
1 tablespoon of tomato paste
4 minced garlic cloves
1/4 teaspoon of turmeric powder
1/2 teaspoon of cumin
1 teaspoon of salt
1/4 teaspoon of pepper
(cumin, salt, and pepper to be adjusted to your taste)

Steps:

1. Add the olive oil, onion, tomato, tomato paste, garlic, and spices to your pan.
2. Stir all the ingredients, cover your pan and cook for 5 minutes on medium heat.
3. Drain the lentils from the water where they were soaked and add them to the pan. Mix all the ingredients well.
4. Add water to your pan until the lentil mixture is covered. Cover your pan and let the lentils cook for 30 minutes on medium heat. Stir from time to time. Check on the water level and add more if necessary. There should always be some sauce in the pan.
5. After 30 minutes, taste the sauce and adjust the salt, pepper, and cumin accordingly.
6. Add the chopped cilantro and parsley to the lentils. Stir well. Cover the pan and cook the lentils for another 10 minutes or until the lentils are done.

Serving:

Serve hot with bread. You can also add some hot sauce if you like spicy food. Enjoy!

Facts:

Lentils are one of the best vegetable sources of proteins and iron and are a great choice for a meat-free, low-fat diet.

Harira

Harira is a traditional Moroccan soup that is served during special occasions, such as the morning after a wedding night. During the holy month of Ramadan, where Muslims fast from dawn until sunset, Moroccans break their fast with this rich soup. Harira is considered a meal in itself and can be served as the main dish for dinner.

Makes: 6 servings; Prep: 15 minutes; Cook: 60 minutes

Ingredients:

2 large tomatoes—peeled and pureed
1 cup meat cubes (optional)
1 onion—chopped
1/3 cup of finely chopped cilantro
1/3 cup of finely chopped parsley
1 celery stick—chopped
2 tablespoons of tomato paste
2 tablespoons of butter
3 teaspoons of salt
1/2 teaspoon of pepper
1 teaspoon of ginger powder

1 can of chickpeas (or 1 cup of dry chickpeas soaked in water over night)
1/2 cup of lentils (soaked in water for 1 hour)
1/3 cup of vermicelli
1/3 cup of flour
2 liters of water

Steps:

1. Add the tomatoes, onion, cilantro, parsley, celery, butter, salt, pepper, ginger powder, lentils, water, and meat (if you want a meat harira) to your cooking pan. Cover the cooking pan and let the ingredients cook for 5 minutes on medium heat. Stir from time to time. ***Note: If you are using dry chickpeas, add them to the other ingredients in step 1. If you are using canned chickpeas, add them towards the end of the cooking time.***
2. After 5 minutes, add water until all the ingredients are covered. Cover the cooking pan and continue cooking the ingredients on medium heat for 45 minutes.
3. After 45 minutes, add the tomato paste to the pan. Mix well with the other ingredients.
4. Dilute the flour with some water. Slowly pour the flour mixture to the harira while stirring.
5. Add the vermicelli. Cover and let the harira cook for another 10 minutes.

Serving:

You can serve the harira with dates. Enjoy!

Variations:

There are several ways of making a traditional harira. Some people like to add meat, while some like to use only vegetables and lentils. You can also substitute rice for the vermicelli pasta to suit your taste. If you like the tang of lemon, add a teaspoon of lemon juice to your bowl!

Vegetable Soup

A good vegetable soup recipe should be in every cook's repertoire. This colorful, creamy soup is a ladle of flavors in a bowl that will make you wonder why you avoided vegetables in your childhood.

Makes: 6 servings; Prep: 15 minutes; Cook: 45 minutes

Ingredients:

2 Leeks
2 Zucchinis
1 Celery Branch
2 Carrots
1 Parsnip
2 Potatoes
1/2 Butternut Squash
A small bunch of Parsley and Cilantro
2/3 cup of light cream
1/2 teaspoon of salt + 1/4 teaspoon of pepper (to be adjusted to your taste)
1.5 liters of water (6 cups)

Steps:

1. Clean, peel, and cut all the vegetables into small pieces.
2. Add all the vegetables, the parsley and cilantro bunch to a cooking pan. Cover with water and cook on medium heat for 40 minutes or until done.
3. Once the vegetables are cooked, remove the bunch of parsley and cilantro from the pan, then transfer the vegetable pieces to a food processor and puree them with the vegetable broth (the water where the vegetables were cooked).
   Note: You can adjust the texture of the soup based on the amount of vegetable broth used to puree the vegetables.
4. Bring back the soup to the cooking pan; add the cream, salt and pepper, and cook on medium hear for another 5 minutes without covering the pan.

Serving:

Serve the soup hot. Enjoy!

Variations:

For a lighter version, you can substitute the heavy cream with light cream or simply omit it from the recipe.

What Is a Tajine?

Moroccan Tajines Made with Clay

A tajine is a traditional Moroccan terracotta pot used to cook Moroccan stews consisting of a combination of meat or poultry and vegetables flavored with spices. Over time, the word 'tajine' started referring to the dish itself in addition to the pot.

The conical shape of the tajine lid causes the steam coming off of the stew to cool down and precipitate back into the vessel. This helps conserve all the aromas of the dish. The meat of the tajine is very tender as it is cooked on a low heat, while the vegetables have the perfect texture as they are layered according to their specific cooking times.

When cooking with traditional tajines, choose one that has a natural brown color and that is lead-free. The ones painted in various colors may contain lead, which can seep into your food and potentially harm your health. You can use the painted tajines for serving and keeping the food warm by placing regular plates containing food inside the tajine.

Do not worry if you do not have a tajine; you can cook all the wonderful Moroccan stews using a cooking pan that you cover with a lid or aluminum foil.

Vegetables Tajine Berber Style

This recipe was traditionally made with a tajine by the Berber people of the Atlas mountains, but then gained popularity in other parts of Morocco given its healthy combination of vegetables and proteins, and ease of preparation.

Makes: 4 servings; Prep: 20 minutes; Cook: 2 hours

Ingredients:

2 tomatoes (sliced)
1 large onion (peeled and sliced)
3 medium potatoes (peeled and cut into cubes)
1 large turnip (peeled and cut into cubes)
3 carrots (peeled and cut into halves)
2 zucchinis (peeled and cut into halves)
1 cup of green peas
1 cup of water
3 tablespoons of olive oil
1 teaspoon of crushed garlic
3 branches of fresh thyme
1 teaspoon of ginger powder

1 tablespoon of rosemary
1/2 teaspoon of turmeric powder
1/4 teaspoon of red chili pepper (to taste)
1 teaspoon of ginger powder
1 teaspoon of salt (to taste)
1/4 teaspoon of pepper (to taste)

Steps:

1. If you are using a tajine to cook this dish make sure that you set the heat on low. However, if you are using a normal cooking pot, you can set the heat to medium.
2. Drizzle the olive oil in your pan, add the onions, and let them cook for 10 minutes.
3. Place the vegetables in the pan. Put the vegetables that take a longer time to cook (potatoes and turnip) in the pan first, and then add the carrots, zucchini, tomatoes, and green peas.
4. Mix all the spices (rosemary, turmeric, chili pepper, ginger, salt, and pepper) in the cup of water. Add the crushed garlic to the water as well. Mix well.
5. Pour the spiced water over the vegetables.
   Note: If you are using a normal cooking pan (instead of a tajine), you may need to adjust the amount of water necessary to cook the vegetables.
6. Cover the tajine and let the vegetables cook for 1 ½ to 2 hours. From time to time, pour some of the sauce over the vegetables on top.
7. Poke the vegetables with a fork to check that they are cooked. The fork should easily cut through the vegetables.
8. When the vegetables are done, remove the lid of the tajine, increase the temperature to medium, and let the sauce thicken for 15 minutes.

Serving:

Serve this tajine with bread. Enjoy!

Variation:

Feel free to substitute any of the vegetables with seasonal ones.

Lamb Tajine with Turnips and Chickpeas

Turnip is a not-so-popular vegetable and many people do not know how to cook it. In Morocco, this tajine of turnips and chickpeas is a very popular homestyle dish that is simple and easy to prepare. Once you taste this tajine, you will see turnips in a new light.

Makes: 4 servings; Prep: 10 minutes; Cook: 50-60 minutes

Ingredients:

1.5 pounds of lamb shoulder (cut into pieces)
6 turnips (peeled and cut into quarters)
1 onion (grated)
15 oz can of chickpeas
1 tablespoon of finely chopped parsley
1 tablespoon of finely chopped cilantro
2 tablespoons of olive oil
1/2 teaspoon of ginger powder
1/4 teaspoon of turmeric powder
A large pinch of saffron

1 teaspoon of salt
1/4 teaspoon of pepper
1 teaspoon of minced garlic
4-6 cups of water

Steps:

1. On medium heat, drizzle the olive oil into your pan. Add the onion, garlic, spices, and meat to the pan. Mix well, cover your pan, and let the meat cook for 10 minutes.
2. After 10 minutes, add 2 cups of water, cover your pan and let the meat cook for 30 minutes. From time to time, stir the meat and check the level of water. Add water, if necessary.
3. When the meat is almost cooked, add the turnips, chickpeas, parsley, and cilantro. Mix well, cover your pan, and let all the ingredients cook for another 20-30 minutes until the meat and turnips are completely cooked. Taste the sauce and adjust the spices as necessary. Also, keep checking the level of water. There should always be some sauce with the tajine.

Serving:

Serve hot with Moroccan bread or French baguette. Enjoy!

Variations:

For variation, you can substitute the turnips with other root vegetables such as potatoes, parsnips or carrots. When doing so, omit the chickpeas.

Lamb Tajine with Almonds

Tajines can also be made with nuts (almonds, walnuts, etc.) and dry fruits (raisins, prunes, apricots, etc.) instead of vegetables. This tajine forms a basis for other tajines of this type. The meaty texture of this dish and the crunchiness of the almonds makes it a winner meal for all meat lovers.

Makes: 4 servings; Prep: 10 minutes; Cook: 50-60 minutes

Ingredients:

1.5 pounds of lamb shoulder (cut into pieces)
2 onions (thinly sliced)
2 tablespoons of olive oil
1 teaspoon of ginger powder
1/4 teaspoon of paprika
A large pinch of saffron
1 teaspoon of salt
1/4 teaspoon of pepper
2 teaspoons of minced garlic
2-3 cups of water

Slivered Almonds
Cooking oil

Steps:

1. On medium heat, drizzle the olive oil into your pan. Add the onions, garlic, spices, and meat. Mix well, cover your pan, and let the meat cook for 10 minutes.
2. After 10 minutes, add 2 cups of water, cover your pan and let the meat cook for 1 hour or until done. From time to time, stir the meat and check on the level of water. Add water if necessary.
3. Set the meat aside and heat the cooking oil in your skillet. Fry the almonds until they become golden brown.
4. Serve the meat topped with the almonds.

Serving:

Serve hot with Moroccan bread or French baguette. Enjoy!

Tips:

Don't have time to cook? This dish can be made the day before, covered and chilled in the refrigerator until you are ready to reheat it and eat. However, keep the almonds separate so that they can stay crunchy when you serve the dish.

double ingredients
triple spices
Olives - green
Lemon -

Mrouzia

Mrouzia is a sweet and savory lamb tajine, or stew, made with raisins and almonds. It is traditionally a dish made during the days of Eid, but it is a fantastic dish to make any time of the year. In the past, the combination of honey and spices helped Moroccan families who had no refrigerator to preserve their meat for a longer time.

Makes: 3-4 servings; Prep: 15 minutes;
Cook: 1 hour and 15 minutes

Ingredients:
1 pound of lamb tender meat or lamb shoulder chops
1 large onion grated
5 Oz of raisins (soaked in water)
4 Oz of blanched almonds
4 Tablespoons of butter
2 Tablespoons of honey
1/2 teaspoon of ginger powder
1/4 teaspoon of pepper (to taste)
1/2 teaspoon of salt (to taste)
1/4 teaspoon of ground cinnamon
A large pinch of saffron
A pinch of turmeric powder
1/2 teaspoon of Ras-El-Hanout
Water

Steps:

1. On medium heat, add the butter, the grated onion, the meat, and the spices to your pan. Mix well, cover the pan and let the meat cook for 5 minutes.
2. Cover the meat with water. Cover the pan and let the meat cook for the next 45 minutes to 1 hour. From time to time, stir the meat and check on the level of water. Add water if necessary.

3. When the meat is almost cooked, drain the raisins from their water and add them to the saucepan. Add the honey.
4. Add a little more water to the meat and raisins if needed.
5. Cover the pan and let the meat and raisins cook for the next 15 minutes.
6. Before serving, heat some cooking oil in your skillet, and fry the almonds until they become golden brown.

Serving:

To serve the Mrouzia, put the meat first on the plate, cover it with the raisins and top it with the almonds. Enjoy!

Tips:

Mrouzia is generally made with lamb meat, but it can also be prepared with beef or goat meat, especially if you want to be careful about the cholesterol component of the lamb.

Important: If you are serving the dish to pregnant women or nursing mothers, make sure to omit Ras-El-Hanout because of some of its components such as lavender leaves.

Chicken Tajine with Carrots and Olives

This tajine is a simple and delicious family meal that is part of every Moroccan family's weekly menu. You can change this dish by adding green peas to the carrots or replacing the olives with pieces of preserved lemons.

Makes: 2 servings; Prep: 15 minutes; Cook: 40 minutes

Ingredients:
1 pound of chicken
1 small onion (finely chopped)
6 carrots (peeled, cut into halves, and cored)
1/4 cup of finely chopped parsley
Green olives
2 tablespoons of olive oil
1/2 teaspoon of ginger powder
1/4 teaspoon of turmeric powder
A large pinch of saffron
1/2 teaspoon of salt (to taste)
1/4 teaspoon of pepper (to taste)
2 cups of water

Steps:

1. On medium heat, drizzle the olive oil into your pan and add the onion, all the spices, and the chicken. Cover your pan and let them cook for 5 minutes.
2. After 5 minutes, add the carrots to the chicken and pour in 2 cups of water.
3. Cover your pan with the lid, and let the chicken cook for 30 minutes.
4. After 30 minutes, check if the chicken is fully cooked by poking it with a fork. The meat should be tender and should not be pink. Add more water if necessary.
5. Add the parsley and olives and cook the chicken for another 5 minutes.

Serving:

Serve this tajine with bread. Enjoy!

Facts:

This dish will help you meet your daily requirement of vegetables. Olives contain monounsaturated fats which can help keep your waistline trim and carrots provide your body with carotene for healthy eyes.

Moroccan Chicken Bastilla

Moroccan Chicken Bastilla is the most popular dish in Morocco, and for good reason. The combination of the layers of savory chicken, eggs, and sweet crunchy almonds makes this dish a favorite for special occasions. Originally, the Bastilla was made with pigeons, but nowadays it is made with chicken, and you can also find multiple other variations such as seafood or other meats.

Makes: 3-4 servings; Prep: 1 hour; Cook: 30 minutes

Ingredients:

Chicken Filling:

1 whole chicken, approximately 2 pounds
2 large onions finely chopped
1 cup of finely chopped parsley
2 tablespoons of cooking oil
1 teaspoon of ginger powder
1 teaspoon of cinnamon powder
1/4 teaspoon of turmeric powder
A large pinch of saffron

1 teaspoon of salt
1/4 teaspoon of pepper
2 cups of water

Eggs Filling:
6 eggs

Almonds Filling:
10 oz of blanched almonds
4 oz of powdered sugar
2 tablespoons of orange blossom water
1/4 of a teaspoon of cinnamon powder
Oil for frying

Dough Ingredients:
Phyllo dough (In Morocco, we use a dough called "Warka")
1 stick of butter (melted)
1 egg yolk

Steps:

Steps to Make the Chicken Filling:

1. On high heat, drizzle the oil into your pan. Add the onions, parsley, and spices. Mix well.
2. Add the whole chicken. Cover your pan and let the chicken cook for 10 minutes.
3. Add just enough water to the chicken for it to cook, since we want a thick sauce. Cover your pan and let the chicken cook for 30 minutes.
4. When the chicken is cooked, remove it from the sauce, let it cool down, and then separate the meat from the bones. Shred the meat into small pieces.

Steps to Make the Eggs Filling:

1. Add the 6 eggs to the sauce where the chicken was cooked.
2. Lower the heat, and stir the eggs into the sauce.
3. Do not cover your pan and let the sauce evaporate. The egg mixture should become dry after 10-15 minutes. Keep stirring from time to time.

Steps to Make the Almonds Filling:

1. Fry the almonds in the oil until they become golden brown.
2. Remove excess oil from the almonds.
3. Process the almonds with the powdered sugar, cinnamon, and orange blossom water in a food processor until the almonds are crushed.

Steps to Fold the Bastilla:

1. Brush your baking pan with melted butter.
2. Fold each piece of the phyllo pastry in half and put 3 layers of folded pastry in the middle of the baking pan. Place folded phyllo pastry sheets around the baking pan so that 1/3 of their length is hanging over the edge of the pan. Brush the phyllo pastry with melted butter.
3. Spread the egg mixture in the middle of the pan. Cover it with 2 layers of phyllo pastry. Brush the phyllo pastry with melted butter.
4. Spread the chicken pieces. Cover them with 2 layers of phyllo pastry. Brush the phyllo pastry with melted butter.
5. Spread the almond mixture. Cover it with 2 layers of phyllo pastry. Brush the phyllo pastry with melted butter. Carefully fold over the phyllo dough on all sides and brush the top of the pastry with melted butter and egg yolk.
6. Add 3-4 layers of phyllo dough pastry on top and tuck them in the bottom of the pie. Brush the surface with melted butter and egg yolk.

Final Steps:

1. Preheat the oven at 350°F and bake the bastilla for 20-30 minutes or until golden brown.
2. Decorate the bastilla with powdered sugar and cinnamon powder before serving.

Serving:

Serve the bastilla hot. Bonne appétit!

Tips:

Phyllo dough is critical for a good bastilla. It is important that you wrap the dough in a damp light kitchen towel to prevent it from becoming dry and breaking apart.

Moroccan Chicken Drumsticks

If you like Southern fried chicken, you'll love this spicy Moroccan version. It is crispy on the outside and tender in the inside, with a little kick of flavor most palettes will enjoy.

Makes: 5 servings; Prep: 5 minutes; Cook: 40 minutes

Ingredients:

5 chicken drumsticks
1 onion (chopped)
1 cup of water
1 tablespoon of cooking oil
1 teaspoon of crushed garlic
1 teaspoon of salt
1 teaspoon of ginger powder
1/4 teaspoon of turmeric powder
1 egg
Bread crumbs
Oil for frying

Steps:

1. Add the cooking oil, onion, chicken, garlic, and spices to your cooking pan. Cover the cooking pan and let all the ingredients cook for 5 minutes on medium heat.
2. After 5 minutes, add 1 cup of water to the chicken. Cover your pan and let the drumsticks cook for 30 minutes. Stir from time to time.
3. Once the chicken is cooked, remove it from the sauce. Reserve the sauce; it will be used with the chicken later.
4. Heat the frying oil in a flat pan.
5. Beat the egg. Dip the chicken drumsticks in the egg, and then coat them with bread crumbs.
6. Fry the chicken drumsticks on every side until golden brown. Use paper towel to remove excess oil when done.

Serving:

Serve the chicken drumsticks immediately with the onion sauce on the side. Enjoy!

Tips:

If you want a healthier option, try this: Omit step 4, and after step five, spray the chicken with canola cooking spray and set on a greased cooking pan. Bake at 300°F, rotating every 10 minutes, until golden.

Calamari with Tomato Sauce

Calamari with tomato sauce is a tasty and healthy dish for calamari lovers. This flavorful and thick red sauce tastes delicious with bread.

Makes: 4 servings; Prep: 15 minutes; Cook: 45 minutes

Ingredients:

1 pound of calamari (squid cut into rings)
2 tomatoes (peeled and pureed)
1/2 onion (chopped)
1/4 cup of finely chopped parsley
1 can of tomato sauce (8 oz)
2 tablespoons of olive oil
1 teaspoon of salt
1/4 teaspoon of pepper
2 teaspoons of paprika

Steps:

1. Add the olive oil, tomatoes, onion, parsley, tomato sauce, salt, pepper, and paprika to your cooking pan. Cover the cooking pan and let all the ingredients cook for 5 minutes on medium heat.
2. Add the calamari to the sauce. Cover your pan and let the calamari cook for 45 minutes to 1 hour. Stir from time to time.

Serving:

Serve the calamari hot with bread or rice. Enjoy!

Tips:

You can also use canned tomatoes instead of fresh, if that is all you have on hand. You can also buy frozen calamari rings if you don't have time to prepare fresh squid.

Shrimp Pil-Pil

Shrimp pil-pil is a Spanish tapas (gambas al pil-pil) that later became a popular appetizer in other Mediterranean countries. In Morocco, this is considered a great dish for parties on warm summer evenings. It is very simple to make and is sure to be a crowd-pleaser since it combines shrimp and a delicious tomato sauce.

Makes: 4 servings; Prep: 10 minutes; Cook: 45 minutes

Ingredients:

16 oz of shrimp (peeled)
5 medium tomatoes
1/4 cup of finely chopped parsley
1/4 cup of finely chopped cilantro
2 tablespoons of olive oil
1 tablespoon of tomato paste
1/2 tablespoon of crushed garlic
1 teaspoon of cumin
1/4 teaspoon of paprika
1 teaspoon of salt
1/4 teaspoon of pepper

Steps:

1. Cut the tomatoes in half and remove the seeds. Grate the inside of the tomatoes into a puree and discard the skin.
2. On medium heat, cook the tomato puree, tomato paste, parsley, cilantro, garlic, olive oil, and all the spices for 15 minutes. Stir the sauce from time to time.
3. Place the shrimp on a baking plate, drizzle the shrimp with some olive oil, and cover it with the tomato sauce.
4. Preheat your oven at 400°F and bake the shrimp for 15-20 minutes or until done.

Serving:

Serve the shrimp hot with crunchy toasted bread.

Variations:

You can also make this recipe using prawns or scallops for a more decadent dish.

Moroccan Sardines with Charmoula

Morocco is the largest sardine exporter in the world, which explains the popularity of sardine dishes in Morocco, where you can find the sardines with charmoula sold by many street vendors. This dish is a great combination of affordability, taste, and health benefits.

Makes: 2 servings; Prep: 20 minutes; Cook: 15 minutes

Ingredients:

Sardine Ingredients:

6 fresh sardines, double filleted or "butterflied"
2 cups of flour
Oil for frying

Charmoula Ingredients:

1/4 cup of finely chopped parsley
1/4 cup of finely chopped cilantro
2 tablespoons of lemon juice

1 tablespoon of olive oil
1/2 tablespoon of minced garlic
1 tablespoon of cumin
1 tablespoon of paprika
1 teaspoon of salt
1/4 teaspoon of pepper

Steps:

1. Prepare the charmoula by mixing all the ingredients of the charmoula together.
2. Place one sardine fillet, skin-side down, on a plate. Cover the surface of the fillet with a couple spoonfuls of charmoula. Cover this layer with another sardine fillet, skin-side up.
3. On high heat, pour the oil onto your pan and let it heat up for 5 minutes. When the oil is hot, reduce the heat.
4. Dredge the stuffed fillets with flour on both sides and fry them in the oil for 5 minutes on each side.
5. Use paper towel to drain the excess oil from the fillets.

Serving:

Serve the sardine fillets immediately. Squeeze some lemon juice on the fillets for additional flavor.

Variation:

For a little kick, add 1/2 teaspoon cayenne pepper to the charmoula before stuffing the fish. This will make the fish extra spicy for those that like hot food.

Tips:

If you want to make the preparation faster you can marinate the fish the day before you plan on cooking them. Simply stuff the fillets with the marinade and place them in an airtight container and store them in the refrigerator until you are ready to use them.

Moroccan Mint Tea

Mint tea is served all day long, traditionally in a special silver pot. If you want an invigorating tea for a hot summer's day, you've found it. This tea practically bursts with cool mint flavor. It can also be served hot for a refreshing twist to teatime. For the best taste, make sure to select young, fresh mint to avoid bitterness.

Makes: 3 cups; Prep: 15 minutes

Ingredients:
3-4 cups of water
A big handful of mint
1 tablespoon of dried green tea
4 tablespoons of sugar

Steps:

1. Boil the water.
2. In a teapot add the mint leaves, dried green tea and sugar.
3. Add the boiled water to the teapot.
4. Mix all the ingredients by pouring tea into a glass and then pouring the tea back into the teapot. Repeat the mixing 2-3 times.

5. Return the teapot to the stove, and on medium heat bring the tea to a boiling point. This is an important step because it allows the sugar to caramelize and give Moroccan tea its special taste.

Variation:

To make a sugar-free version of this tea, you can either omit sugar, or add two packets of calorie-free sweetener to the tea instead of sugar. You may want to try adding a few drops of orange blossom water to this recipe before serving for a little added flavor.

Quick Tip:

To make this tea extra-special, garnish your tea glasses with sprigs of fresh mint.

Moroccan Teapot

Summer juices with Moroccan Twist

Make a warm summer day more enjoyable by trying one of these drinks. What's the Moroccan twist? Each juice incorporates orange blossom water. Orange blossom water comes from the steam distillation used to make essential oil from Seville orange blossoms. It is considered a gourmet ingredient, known for its therapeutic purposes, and adds a touch of Morocco to any drink.

Makes: 1 serving each; Prep: 5 minutes each

Almond Milk

Almond Milk Ingredients:

1/4 teaspoon of orange blossom water
3/4 cup of cold milk
1/4 cup of water
1/2 cup of whole almonds
1/2 tablespoon of sugar

Almond Milk Steps:

1. Mix all the ingredients together in a blender.
2. Sift the juice to get rid of the solid almond mix.
3. Serve cold.

Peach Juice

Peach Juice Ingredients:
1/4 teaspoon of orange blossom water
1 cup of orange juice
2 peaches cut into pieces
1 tablespoon of lemon juice
sugar to taste

Peach Juice Steps:

1. Mix all the ingredients together in a blender.
2. Serve cold.

Watermelon Juice

Watermelon Juice Ingredients:
1/4 teaspoon of orange blossom water or rose water
Frozen watermelon
some water
sugar to taste

Watermelon Steps:

1. Mix all the ingredients together in a blender.
2. Serve cold.

Tips:

Instead of blending or serving your juice drinks with ice, you can alternatively freeze your fruits before using them in the juice recipe.

Ginger Juice

Fresh ginger is good for treating nausea caused by sea-sickness and morning sickness. Some people also use it as a remedy for colds. This ginger juice is a refreshing blend of taste and health!

Makes: 4 servings; Prep: 5 minutes

Ingredients:

4 cups of water
15 oz of pineapple
2 oz of fresh ginger
1/3 cup of lemon juice
6 tablespoons of sugar

Steps:

1. Blend all the ingredients together in a blender.
2. Filter the juice using a sifter. Discard the pulp caught in the sifter.
3. Pour the filtered juice in a pitcher for serving.

Serving:

Serve cold. Enjoy!

Quick Tip:

Frozen ginger is easier to grate. To freeze ginger, wrap it tightly in plastic wrap and put in the freezer overnight. When you are ready to use it simply unwrap the root of ginger and grate it as you normally would.

Msemmen

Msemmen is a Moroccan flaky crêpe that is traditionally served with Moroccan tea for breakfast or afternoon snack. It is often topped with honey and butter and resembles a very flat pancake, though a properly cooked msemmen will flake apart as you eat it, unlike a pancake.

Makes: 8-10 msemmen; Prep: 45 minutes;
Cook: 5-10 minutes in each side on low heat

Ingredients:
2 cups of flour
1 cup of semolina
3/4 cup of oil
3 tablespoons of butter
1 tablespoon of salt
1 tablespoon of sugar
1 teaspoon of dry yeast
1-2 cups of warm water (depending on the quality of absorption of your flour)

Steps:

Steps for making the dough:

1. Mix all the dry ingredients together (flour, semolina, salt, sugar, and yeast).
2. Slowly add warm water and work the dough until you are able to create a ball with the dough.
3. If you are kneading the dough by hand, use energetic and quick strokes. Knead for 20 minutes while adding water until you get elastic-like dough. You can use a kneading machine to speed up the process if you

like. To use a kneading machine, put the dough ball in the machine and let it automatically knead for the next 10 minutes as you add water.

4. Make small balls with the dough (the size of golf balls) and let the dough rest for 20 minutes.

Note: The amount of water needed depends on the quality of absorption of the flour you are using. The goal is to get an elastic and malleable dough. If your dough is too sticky add some flour; if it is too hard add some water and continue kneading it.

Steps for folding the Msemmen:

1. Mix the melted butter with the oil.
2. Spread some of the oil/butter mixture on your hands and flat work surface.
3. Take one dough ball and flatten it with your hands. Gently keep stretching the dough until you get a think circle of dough.
4. Rub some oil on top, and fold the left and right sides into the middle, one side on top of the other, to obtain a rectangular shape.
5. Sprinkle some semolina and some oil on the strip. Fold again the left and right sides into the middle, one side on top of the other, to obtain a square shape.
6. Repeat steps 3-5 with the remaining balls.

Steps for cooking the Msemmen:

1. Heat up a skillet and add a small amount of oil to it.
2. Gently spread the dough square with your fingertips until it stretches and becomes thin, but should remain in a square shape.
3. On low heat, cook the msemmen 5-10 minutes in each side until it becomes golden brown.

Note: Make sure to use enough of the oil/butter mixture at all steps; otherwise, the dough will rip or will not cook correctly.

Serving:

The msemmen is served hot with honey and Moroccan mint tea.

Variations:

Before folding the msemmen, you can stuff it with different items to add extra flavors. The fillings may consist of cooked ground meat, cooked onions, or sweetened ground almonds.

Harcha

Harcha is a pan-fried bread that is a popular Morocco teatime and breakfast staple. It looks a lot like an English muffin, but has a graininess that may remind you of cornbread.

Makes: 6 portions; Prep: 5 minutes;
Cook: 15-20 minutes

Ingredients:
2 cups of semolina
1 cup of water
1/2 cup of canola oil
1/2 tablespoons of baking powder
1 teaspoon of sugar
½ teaspoon of salt

Steps for making the dough:

1. Mix the semolina, baking powder, sugar, and salt together.
2. Gradually add the oil to the dry mixture as you are working the semolina with your hands.
3. Slowly add the water to the mixture until you get a paste. The amount of water may vary depending on the absorption quality of your semolina.
4. Form a ball with the dough and sprinkle it with extra semolina.
5. Sprinkle some semolina on a warm pan and transfer the dough to the pan. Flatten the dough with your fist to get a disk.
6. Cook the harcha on one side for 10 minutes, then use a plate to flip it and transfer it back to the pan to cook it on the other side. Keep flipping the harcha until it is fully cooked and becomes golden brown.

Serving:

Serve harcha warm with jam, butter and honey, cheese, or any filling of your choice. Enjoy!

Variations:

For a sweeter taste you can add three tablespoons of sugar or honey to the batter. This sweeter harcha can be eaten like pancakes with your favorite syrup or a drizzle of honey. In this recipe, the harcha was shaped as a pan-sized disk of dough. You can also shape it as individual size small round disks.

Amlou

In Berber households, Amlou is served as a breakfast time dip for bread. It is similar to almond butter as it is primarily made from almonds and Argan oil.

Makes: 1 jar of Amlou; Prep: 40 minutes

Ingredients:
10 oz of unsalted raw Almonds
10 oz of Argan oil
Honey (to taste)

Steps:
1. Roast the almonds in the oven to 400°F for 20-30 minutes.
2. Grind the almonds until you get a a fine almond powder.
3. Add the argan oil and the honey to the almond powder. Mix well with a spoon.
   Note: To get a thinner consistency of Amlou, add more argan oil. Adjust the sweetness of Amlou to your taste by adjusting the amount of honey.

Serving:

Amlou is traditionally served as a dip with bread, and accompanied with mint tea. You can also use it as a filling for crepes.

Variations:

If you do not like almonds, subsitute with raw peanuts and follow the exact same steps!

Moroccan Almond Macaroons

In Morocco, cookies and pastries are mainly made of almonds and flavored with orange blossom water, which makes them a perfect complement to Moroccan mint tea. The smooth texture and soft flavors of these hand made almond cookies will, for sure, add them to your list of favorite snacks.

Makes: 20 macaroons; Prep: 15 minutes; Cook: 15 minutes

Ingredients:

12 oz of whole almonds
6 oz of powdered sugar
2 eggs
1 small lemon
1 teaspoon of baking powder
1 tablespoon of cooking oil for rolling
Whole almonds for decoration

Steps:

1. Grind the almonds in a grinder until you get an almond powder with a fine texture.
2. Grate the peel of the lemon to get the lemon zest.
3. Separate the egg yolks from the egg whites.
4. Mix the egg yolks with the almond powder, powdered sugar, lemon zest, and the baking powder.
5. Beat the egg whites until you obtain a thick, white foam.
6. Incorporate the egg whites in the egg yolks mixture. Use your hand to mix the dough to ensure that all ingredients are well incorporated.
7. To roll the macaroons, put some cooking oil in your hands so that the dough does not stick to them. Take a small amount of the dough and roll it in a ball, flatten it a bit, and place it in a baking pan with wax paper.
8. Preheat your oven to 350°F and bake the macaroons for 15 minutes.

Note: Do not over-bake the cookies. When still hot, the macaroons are very soft; however, as they cool down, their texture changes and gets chewier.

Variations:

For a chewier cookie, add 1 tablespoon of butter to the recipe and 8 oz of powdered sugar instead of 6 oz. You can also add a teaspoon of vanilla for a smoother flavor.

Quick Tip:

You can freeze these cookies for up to three months in an airtight container.

M'Hanncha

M'Hanncha is a Moroccan almond pastry that is often called an Almond Snake Pastry because of the way it is twisted into a coil before it is baked. In fact, M'Hanncha literally means "coiled like a snake." This decadent dessert , filled with almond paste and dipped in honey, makes a delicious treat your family and friends won't forget.

Makes: 4-6 servings; Prep: 30 minutes; Cook: 30-40 minutes

Ingredients for the Filling:
9 oz Blanched almonds
4 oz Sugar
1 Tablespoon butter
2 Tablespoons orange blossom water
1/4 Teaspoon ground cinnamon

Ingredients for the Pastry:
Phyllo dough
1 Stick butter (melted)
1 Egg yolk

Ingredients for Decorations:
Honey
Orange blossom water
Fried almonds

Steps:

1. To make the filling, mix all of the filling ingredients together with a food processor to make an almond paste. Remove the mixture from the food processor and manually mix it with a spoon. Repeat this process several times until the almonds are no longer visible in the mixture and you have a smooth paste.
2. Roll the almond paste into thin tubes as long as a sheet of phyllo dough.
3. Place three sheets of phyllo dough on your counter and brush the top sheet with butter.
4. Place one of your almond paste tubes on one side of the sheets of phyllo dough.
5. Roll the almond paste tube in the phyllo dough.
6. Using your index fingers, gently push each end of the roll to close the phyllo dough around the almond paste. Repeat steps 3-6 until all of the almond paste is wrapped in phyllo dough.
7. Brush a round baking pan with melted butter and then coil the almond rolls inside of the pan.
8. Brush the finished roll with melted butter. Add some water to the egg yolk and brush the top of the coils with the water and yolk mixture.
9. Preheat your oven to 350°F and bake the coil for 30-40 minutes or until golden brown.
10. To make the honey syrup, melt the honey on low heat in a pan and flavor it with some orange blossom water.
11. Pour the syrup over the baked M'Hanncha, then sprinkle the fried almonds on top.

Serving:

Serve the M'Hanncha cold with Moroccan mint tea.

Variations:

You can substitute rose water for orange blossom water if you like and finish the treat with a sprinkling of cinnamon and powdered sugar instead of the honey syrup. The M'Hanncha can also be fried in butter instead of baked.

Quick Tip:

Make sure to cover the phyllo dough with a damp cloth while it sits on the counter or it will become brittle.

Date Almond Truffles

These date almond truffles are flour-free, which makes them a wonderful treat for those with gluten allergies. Also, they do not require any baking, which makes them a fantastic dessert for those days when you crave a sweet snack but do not want to spend time in the kitchen!

Makes: 20 truffles; Prep: 30 minutes

Ingredients:

2 cups of pitted dates
2 cups blanched slivered almonds
Natural unsweetened shredded coconut
2 tablespoons of honey
1 tablespoon of orange blossom water
½ teaspoon of cinnamon powder

Steps for making the dough:

1. Steam the dates, over boiling water, for 20 minutes.
2. On medium heat, roast the almonds in a pan till they become golden brown. Stir from time to time.
3. Pour the almonds and dates into a food processor and blend together until you get a thick paste.
4. When done, add honey, cinnamon, and orange blossom water to the paste and mix with your hands.
5. Make balls from the paste the size of walnuts and roll them in the shredded coconut.

Serving:

Serve the truffles cold. Enjoy!

Variations:

Instead of honey, coconut, orange blossom water, and cinnamon powder, you can use the finely grated rind of a lime, 2 tsp cacao powder or carob powder, and the juice squeezed from half of the lime. This will add a tang to the truffles.

This recipe shapes the dessert as bite-sized balls, but you can be creative in trying different shapes if you like.